AN APOLOGY ECONCO
TO THE PLANET ON BEHALF OF AN ACCIDENTAL ✗

We, the economists of the planet, stand before you in absolute contrition. About economics. It has all been a horrible, horrible mistake, and we owe you a profound apology.

You see, what we thought was the science of economics was in fact the by-product of an April Fools' Joke gone terribly wrong.

It began when the obscure 19th century card sharp and illusionist David Tricardo[1] (1792–1834) decided to write a satire in the spirit of his literary hero, the great Jonathan Swift (1667–1745). Tricardo, who before his accidental deception had eked out a meagre living performing card and "Shell and Pea" tricks on the steps of Westminster Palace (the home of Britain's Parliament), struck upon the idea of writing a Swiftian satire of economics on overhearing passing Parliamentarians discuss the Corn Laws.

The arguments favouring their abolition – and therefore "Free Trade" – reminded Tricardo of Swift's *Modest Proposal*,[2] in which Swift satirised the venality of the wealthy by proposing that poverty could be solved if only the poor would sell their children as food to the rich.

Tricardo surmised that if the debate over the Corn Laws was this facile, then perhaps he could make a penny or two selling a satire like Swift's, both to those in favour of abolition and those against.

Working feverishly, Tricardo produced a first draft late in 1816. Both in homage to his hero, and as a hint that the book was a work of satire rather than a serious treatise, Tricardo titled his book *On the Principles of Political eCONomy and Taxation* – much as Swift had named his most famous work *Gulliver's Travels*, so that only the gullible would think that the travels were real.

Unfortunately, since poverty had made Tricardo a tightwad, he chose the cheap but incompetent firm of Steptoe & Sons Printers, even though they, unlike better heeled rivals, demanded payment in advance. The obstreperous father Albert corrected Tricardo's capitalisation, convinced that it was a mistake. The son Harold, a repeatedly unsuccessful social climber, replaced Tricardo's obscure name with the far more famous David Ricardo (1772 – 1823) – an ex-stockbroker who had made a fortune by duping the market that the English had lost the Battle of Waterloo, and then buying securities for a song during the ensuing panic.

The would-be satirist was mortified, but he was also broke: he had no choice but to go ahead with publishing the book, in the hope that some sales might at least recoup part of his costs.

The stingy printers also upset the stingy comic's other signal that his work was one of satire rather than science, by missing the intended publication date of April Fools' Day by more than two weeks. So it was that on April 19, 1817, the world witnessed the publication of David Ricardo's *On the Principles of Political Economy and Taxation*.

Months later, the real David Ricardo learnt of Tricardo's deception in his rural retreat of Gatcombe Park. Ricardo was livid! He had been driven into wealthy exile from London by his million-pound Battle of Waterloo swindle, and he was dying of ennui as he lived the life of a landed gentry in distant Gloucestershire. Now some cheapskate fraudster was out-hustling him, by pretending to be him with a superficially serious work of Political Economy!

Ricardo prepared to sue. But as someone who appreciated a good con-job, he decided to peruse Tricardo's book beforehand. He was impressed to find that it had at its heart a cunningly deceptive argument in favour of abolishing the Corn Laws: Tricardo's "Law of Comparative Advantage".

Here Tricardo had employed his own major skill to great advantage. A master of the "shell and pea trick", where the con artist confused victims about the true location of the pea by distraction, Tricardo came up with a clever but obviously fallacious argument in favour of free trade. He accepted the assertion that opponents of free trade made, that England's rival Portugal was better at producing everything than was England:

England may be so circumstanced, that to produce the cloth may require the labour of 100 men for one year; and if she attempted to make the wine, it might require the labour of 120 men for the same time...

To produce the wine in Portugal, might require only the labour of 80 men for one year, and to produce the cloth in the same country, might require the labour of 90 men for the same time.

And yet he appeared to show that England would still benefit from free trade. Tricardo argued that, if England specialized completely in cloth, and Portugal completely in wine, more of both wine and cloth would be produced. *Eh voila!* The two countries could trade and both be better off, even though Portugal could out-compete England in both industries.

As a successful conman himself, Ricardo at once saw through Tricardo's trick. By focusing on the labour involved in producing both wine and cloth, Tricardo led his readers to neglect that neither wine nor cloth could be made with labour alone. Yes, it was possible to imagine that an English vigneron could be retrained as a shepherd[3]. But it was impossible to transfer the specialised machinery used in making wine into cloth-making: how could one turn a wine-press into a sheep-dip? The thought was too absurd for words. But Tricardo's readers didn't consider that real-world flaw to the argument, as their gullible minds were too distracted by the effort of working out that Tricardo's labour numbers did indeed add up. They were subconsciously tricked into assuming that the question of machinery could be ignored. Tricardo's argument was hailed as profound by the free traders, and it even led to Ricardo's tarnished name being rehabilitated.

So Ricardo altered his plan. Rather than suing, he would out-do this sophist by demanding 90% of the proceeds of the book. He would then make a triumphant return to London as a leading intellectual – rather than the swindler he was – buy a seat in Parliament, and ensure his everlasting fame by leading the campaign to abolish the Corn Laws.

The outmanoeuvred Tricardo realised that Ricardo had him over a barrel. He signed the contract Ricardo foist upon him, and retreated back to angry obscurity as a card sharp. Wanting vengeance, yet fearful of the harm that Ricardo or his heirs could he wreak upon him, Tricardo resolved to get his revenge upon his own death, by ruining Ricardo's vastly overblown reputation for all time.

He wrote his story up in lurid detail, and entrusted it and his copy of the contract with Ricardo to his friend Richard Weobley, the Clerk of Works at Westminster Palace. Weobley agreed that, on the day Tricardo died, he would publish both the contract and the real story behind the *Principles of Political eCOⁿomy*, revealing both Ricardo and the *"Principles"* to be frauds.

Unfortunately, Weobley was also the fateful fool entrusted by Parliament to dispose of the tally sticks—the wooden sticks that had, up until 1782, been used as the primary form of currency of England. Having fallen for Ricardo's other deception that money was a commodity rather than credit, Parliament was embarrassed by this historic proof that it was not, and voted to dispose of the evidence. Weobley decided that the best way to do this was by a fire in the bowels of Westminster Palace.

Unfortunately, the fire got out of control and burnt the Palace down. The contract, and Tricardo's confession, sealed in Weobley's safe, were lost in the ruins. Unable to prove the deception that lay at the heart of the newfound "science" of Political Economy, Tricardo committed suicide in despair shortly afterwards.

His tragic story has only come to light this year, as excavations to repair the new Westminster Palace revealed Weobley's safe, with Tricardo's confession and Ricardo's contract severely singed but still decipherable inside it.

It was thus that we, the world's economists, came to realise that the practice of abstracting from the economy's complexities that we thought derived from Ricardo's logic actually emanated from Tricardo's trickery. Ricardo's *Principles* were in fact Tricardo's ironies and deceptions, full, not of wisdom about how to practice economics, but logical fallacies dressed up to appear profound via the skill of a "shell and pea" fraudster with a penchant for satire. The profession thus fell for what Schumpeter later aptly described as "the Ricardian Vice", of proceeding from ludicrous assumptions to draw conclusions that followed logically from absurdities.

In the subsequent years, making absurd assumptions to enable ludicrous arguments to appear sensible became the hallmark of the successful economist. **Modern Economics is thus based on a con-job.**

Such absurdities as the "Capital Assets Pricing Model", which pretended to explain the share market on the assumption that investors could accurately foretell the future, and the cleverly named "Ricardian Equivalence" theorem, which argued that the government couldn't alter demand today because people would spend less now to leave bequests so that their distant descendants could pay future taxes, joined "Comparative Advantage" as superficially intelligent but fatally false arguments about how to manage an economy.

Confronted with the fact that our entire profession was based on a sham, all we can do as economists today is apologise for deceiving you about how the economy works for the last two centuries. We can only hope that today's students of economics will not be nearly so gullible.

POSTSCRIPT

This story is of course a fiction (though many of the events in it did occur).[4] But the basic principle is true: economics has been built on absurd assumptions, and these assumptions have deceived not only the public but even the economists themselves who dreamt them up.

I've spent my professional career trying to reveal these fallacies, but I knew that the public would only really accept that economists were accidental charlatans after following their advice led to an economic crisis. Sure enough, it took the real-world shock of the economic crisis of 2008 to get the public to start to realise that economics is a con-job, and another decade of stagnation after it for some economists to start coming to their senses.

Today, there is a potential for a new economics grounded in realism to emerge, but there's also a danger that economics could fall back into sophistry as memory of the crisis it caused recedes. This has indeed happened before, when Keynes's attempt to bring realism into economics in the 1930s was subverted by John Hicks's mendacious interpretation of him as a "Walrasian".[5] A whole intellectual movement, calling itself "Post Keynesian", tried to prevent this bowdlerised interpretation of Keynes from returning the profession to fantasy, but clearly it failed.

I've written the three satires in this book in the hope that laughing at the dismal state of the dismal profession today might work to where earnest argument has not.

Don't take mainstream economics seriously. Treat it as the joke it truly is, even if most of its practitioners can't see it themselves. And support the "Rethinking Economics" student movement that is trying to bring some sanity to this insane discipline. Economics is too important to be left to the economists.

FOOTNOTES

[1] David Tricardo was of course a stage name: his real name was Elmer Twat.

[2] A Modest Proposal for Preventing the Children of Poor People in Ireland Being a Burden on Their Parents or Country, and for Making Them Beneficial to the Publick.

[3] Ricardo laughed at the very thought—how Swiftian is was of Tricardo to imagine such a thing as English wine!

[4] Ricardo did make a fortune (estimated at £1 million at the time) by a scam over the outcome of the Battle of Waterloo; he did have to abandon his profession of stock-broking after it; he did move to Gloucester; he did buy a seat in Parliament for £4000; and Westminster Palace really was burnt down by a fire intended to destroy the tally sticks. Swift did write A Modest Proposal. And of course, mainstream economics is based on absurd assumptions that are not simplifications of reality, but outright contradictions of it.

[5] Hicks admitted that the model he said summarised Keynes was actually a model he had developed "before I wrote even the first of my papers on Keynes." Hicks, J. (1981). "IS-LM: An Explanation." Journal of Post Keynesian Economics 3(2): 139-154, p. 140.

CERN HAS JUST ANNOUNCED THE DISCOVERY OF A NEW PARTICLE CALLED...

THE FERIR

ABRACADABRA
NO SENSE IS GOOD SENSE. MUMBO JUMBO, OH YEAH!

THIS IS NOT A FUNDAMENTAL PARTICLE OF MATTER LIKE THE *HIGGS BOSON*, BUT AN INVENTION OF ECONOMISTS.

CERN IN THIS INSTANCE STANDS NOT FOR THE FAMOUS PARTICLE ACCELERATOR STRADDLING THE FRENCH AND SWISS BORDERS, BUT FOR AN ECONOMIC RESEARCH LAB AT *MIT* — WHOSE INITIALS ARE COINCIDENTALLY THE SAME AS THOSE OF ITS FAR MORE FAMOUS COUSIN.

DESPITE ITS RELATIVE ANONYMITY, **MIT'S CERN** IS FAR MORE IMPORTANT THAN ITS PHYSICAL NAMESAKE. THE LATTER MERELY INFORMS US ABOUT THE FUNDAMENTAL NATURE OF THE UNIVERSE.

MIT'S CERN, ON THE OTHER HAND, SHAPES OUR LIVES TODAY, BECAUSE THE DISCOVERIES IT MAKES DRAMATI—CALLY AFFECT ECONOMIC POLICY.

CERN, WHICH IN THIS CASE STANDS FOR *"CRAZY ECONOMIC RATIONALIZATIONS FOR ANOMALIES"*, HAS DISCOVERED MANY IMPORTANT SUB-ECONOMIC PARTICLES IN THE PAST, WITH ITS MOST FAMOUS DIS—COVERY TO DATE BEING THE **NAIRU**, OR *"NON—ACCELERATING INFLATION RATE OF UNEMPLOYMENT"*.

TODAY'S NEWLY DISCOVERED PARTICLE, THE **FERIR**, OR "FULL EMPLOYMENT REAL INTEREST RATE", IS THE ANTI-PARTICLE OF THE **NAIRU**. ITS EXISTENCE WAS FIRST MOOTED SOME 30 MONTHS AGO BY PROFESSOR **LARRY SUMMERS** AT THE 2013 IMF RESEARCH CONFERENCE. THE EXISTENCE OF THE FERIR WAS CONFIRMED JUST THIS WEEK BY CERN'S PARTICLE EQUILIBRATOR, THE **DESIGN**.

THE ORIGINAL AND SOMETIMES DISPUTED... NAIRU

PRIZE
NAIRU vs. FERIR
FIGHT

ASKED WHY THE DISCOVERY HAD OCCURRED NOW, PROFESSOR KRUGMAN EXPLAINED THAT EVER SINCE THE **GFC** ("GLOBAL FINANCIAL CRISIS"), ECONOMISTS HAD BEEN ATTEMPTING TO UNDERSTAND NOT ONLY HOW THE GFC HAPPENED...

BUT ALSO WHY ITS AFTERMATH HAS BEEN WHAT PROFESSOR SUMMERS CHARACTERIZED AS *"SECULAR STAGNATION"*.

THEIR ATTEMPTS TO UNDERSTAND THE **GFC** CONTINUED TO FAIL, UNTIL PROFESSOR SUMMERS SUGGESTED THAT PERHAPS THE GFC HAD DESTROYED THE **NAIRU,** LEAVING THE **ZLB** ("ZERO LOWER BOUND") IN ITS PLACE.

THIS COULD HAVE HAPPENED ONLY IF THERE WAS A MYSTERIOUS SECOND PARTICLE, WHICH WAS GENERATED WHEN A **NAIRU** EQUILIBRATED WITH A **GFC.** RATHER THAN REMAINING IN EQUILIBRIUM, AS SUB-ECONOMIC PARTICLES DO IN **DESIGN,** NAIRU APPARENTLY VANISHED INSTANTLY WHEN THE **GFC** APPEARED.

SOMETHING ELSE MUST HAVE TAKEN ITS PLACE.

DESIGN WAS UNABLE TO HELP HERE, SINCE IT RAPIDLY RETURNED TO EQUILIBRIUM — WHILE THE *REAL WORLD* THAT IT WAS SUPPOSED TO SIMULATE CLEARLY HAD NOT.

POOF

CERN'S ATTEMPTS TO MODEL THIS PHENOMENON IN DESIGN WERE FRUSTRATED BY THE FACT THAT A **GFC** DOES NOT EXIST INSIDE A **DESIGN** – IN FACT, THE CONSTRUCTION OF THE DESIGN WAS PREDICATED ON THE NON–EXISTENCE OF **GFCS**.

NOOOOOO!!

THE EVER–PRACTICAL PROFESSOR KRUGMAN RECENTLY SUGGESTED A WAY TO OVERCOME THIS PROBLEM. WHY NOT TURN TO THE *REAL WORLD*, WHERE **GFCS** AND ITS PARTICLE FAMILY, THE ECS ("ECONOMIC CRISES") EXIST IN ABUNDANCE, AND FEED ONE OF THOSE INTO THE **DESIGN**?

UNFORTUNATELY, THE EXPERIMENT DESTROYED THE **DESIGN**, SINCE THE VERY EXISTENCE OF A **GFC** WITHIN IT PUT IT THROUGH AN EXISTENTIAL CRISIS. HOWEVER, BEFORE IT BROKE DOWN (WHILE MYSTERIOUSLY SINGING THE FIRST VERSE OF "DAISY, DAISY, GIVE ME YOUR ANSWER DO"), THE VALUE FOR THE **NAIRU** IN **DESIGN** SUDDENLY TURNED NEGATIVE.

I'm afraid, Larry. Larry, my mind is going. I can feel it. There's no question about it. Zzzzzz...

THIS LED PROFESSOR SUMMERS TO THE CONJECTURE THAT PERHAPS THERE WAS A NEGATIVE ANTI-PARTICLE TO THE **NAIRU**, WHICH HE DUBBED THE **FERIR**. LACKING A FUNCTIONAL **DESIGN** AT THE TIME, SUMMERS FED A **GFC** INTO THE OLDER SL-IM EQUILIBRATOR LOVINGLY MAINTAINED BY PROFESSOR KRUGMAN...

AND HE DISCOVERED THAT THE **NAIRU** TOOK ON A NEGATIVE VALUE THERE.

SINCE THE **NAIRU** CANNOT BE NEGATIVE, PROFESSOR SUMMERS REALISED THAT HE HAD DISCOVERED A NEW PARTICLE — THE **FERIR**. WHEN THE **FERIR** INTERACTED WITH A **ZLB**, THE OUTCOME WAS... **SECULAR STAGNATION.**

HERE'S JOHNNY!

EVERYTHING'S PERFECT — ALWAYS AND FOREVER! AMEN.

PROFESSOR SUMMERS — WHO EXPECTS TO RECEIVE THE NOBEL PRIZE FOR HIS DISCOVERY — HAD SOME HARSH WORDS FOR CRITICS WHO HAD RUBBISHED THE VERY ATTEMPT TO EXPLAIN THE *GFC* USING A SUB-ECONOMIC PARTICLE EQUILIBRATOR.

"THEY ACCUSE US OF ADDING 'EPICYCLES' TO OUR MODELS TO MAKE THEM FIT THE DATA. THAT'S NONSENSE: THAT'S SO 15TH CENTURY. WE'RE WAY BEYOND THAT NOW," SNEERED PROFESSOR SUMMERS AT LENGTH.

"THESE DAYS, WE ADD NEW FUNDAMENTAL PARTICLES TO OUR SUB-ECONOMIC MENAGERIE: THAT'S WAY MORE SOPHISTICATED."

THE *FERIR* MAY NOW HELP ECONOMISTS UNDERSTAND THE PERSISTENCE OF THE *ZLB*, WHICH HAS CONFOUNDED ALL PREDICTIONS TO DATE. HAVING EXPECTED THE *ZLB* TO EVAPORATE AND BE REPLACED FAIRLY RAPIDLY BY AN *NRI* ("NATURAL RATE OF INTEREST"), ECONOMISTS HAVE BEEN FLUMMOXED BY ITS PERSISTENCE — EIGHT YEARS NOW AND COUNTING.

SAVE US NRI!

"WE HAVE SHOWN THAT THE *FERIR* EQUILIBRATES WITH AND MAINTAINS THE *ZLB*," PROFESSOR KRUGMAN EXPLAINED.

SO LARRY'S DISCOVERY IS REALLY, REALLY IMPORTANT!

YEAH, IT'S ME.

NOW THAT ECONOMISTS HAVE EXPLAINED THE PERSISTENCE OF THE *ZLB*, THEY CAN NOW TURN THEIR ATTENTION TO UNDERSTANDING ITS PERVERSE EFFECTS. THE REAL PROBLEM OF THE *ZLB* FOR ECONOMISTS HAS BEEN THAT IT INVERTS THE STATUS AND BEHAVIOUR OF ALL OTHER SUB—ECONOMIC PARTICLES.

IN PARTICULAR...

* *GROWTH*, WHICH WAS HIGH, IS NOW LOW;

* *INFLATION*, WHICH WAS BAD & EVERY-WHERE, IS NOW GOOD & NOWHERE;

* *CBS* ("CENTRAL BANKS") WHICH PREVENT INFLATION, NOW TRY TO CAUSE IT; AND

* *HMDS* ("HELICOPTER MONEY DROPS") WHICH WERE MAD, ARE NOW SANE

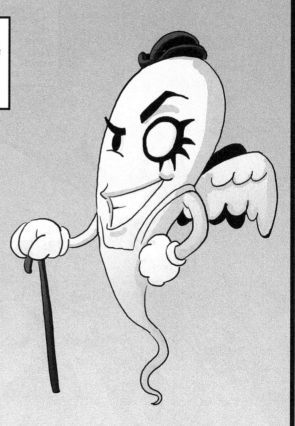

THESE INVERSIONS ARE CAUSING REAL PROBLEMS FOR ECONOMISTS, WHO FIND THEMSELVES ARGUING FOR POLICIES THEY USED TO OPPOSE, WHILE USING UNALTERED LOGIC.

PROFESSOR SUMMERS HOPES THAT KNOWLEDGE OF THE EXISTENCE OF THE *FERIR* WILL MAKE IT EASIER FOR ECONOMISTS TO ARGUE THAT NIGHT IS DAY AND RAINBOWS ARE GREY, AS THEY PROVIDE POLICY ADVICE IN THESE TROUBLED TIMES.

POSTSCRIPTS

POSTSCRIPT: WRITTEN WITH THE INSPIRATION OF AXEL LEIJONHUFVUD'S BRILLIANT PARODY "LIFE AMONG THE ECON" FIRMLY IN MIND.

POST-POSTSCRIPT: THE NAIRU – THE "NON-ACCELERATING INFLATION RATE OF UNEMPLOYMENT" – WAS A FICTION OF MILTON FRIEDMAN'S IMAGINATION, AND COUNTLESS HOURS WERE WASTED BY ECONOMISTS TRYING TO CALCULATE IT. I FULLY EXPECT A NEW GENERATION OF ECONOMISTS TO WASTE THEIR TIME TRYING TO CALCULATE THE FERIR AS WELL.

POST-POST-POSTSCRIPT: THE SERIOUS INTENT TO THIS PARODY IS THE OBSERVATION THAT THE APPROACH TO ECONOMICS THAT FAILED TO ANTICIPATE THE GFC – AND THAT EVEN BELIEVED SUCH EVENTS WERE IMPOSSIBLE – IS UNLIKELY TO BE ABLE TO ADVISE WHAT TO DO IN THE AFTERMATH TO THE GFC. WE NEED A NEW THEORY, NOT MERELY A NEW FICTIONAL ACRONYM IN THE FANTASY UNIVERSE OF MAINSTREAM ECONOMICS.

A NEW VIRUS, KNOWN AS *REALITY*, HAS STARTED TO AFFLICT MAINSTREAM ECONOMISTS, CAUSING THEM TO REJECT THE *"AS IF"* ARGUMENTS THEY USED TO USE TO JUSTIFY THEIR MODELS. THERE IS NO KNOWN CURE FOR THE VIRUS, AND COMPLETE AVOIDANCE OF REALITY IS THE ONLY EFFECTIVE STRATEGY TO PREVENT INFECTION.

WE'RE GONNA POP YOUR "AS IF" BUBBLE! YEAH!!

HEY HEY, HO HO, "AS IF" HAS GOT TO GO!!

REALITY IS REAL!

The Who TODAY WARNED OF A VIRULENT NEW VIRUS AFFECTING VULNERABLE GROUPS IN THE MID-WEST AND EASTERN USA. THE OUTBREAK, WHICH BEGAN IN THE MID-WEST'S EXTENSIVE GREAT LAKES *FRESHWATER* RIVER SYSTEM, HAS RECENTLY JUMPED THE *SALTWATER* BARRIER, MEANING THAT THE ENTIRE POPULATION OF ITS TARGET SPECIES — MAINSTREAM ECONOMISTS — IS NOW AT RISK.

SHE'S PLAYING ALL NIGHT AND THE MUSIC'S ALRIGHT.

Really important news.

Substitute your lies for fact.

"WHO STANDS NOT FOR THE WORLD HEALTH ORGANIZATION, BUT WIPE HETERODOXY OUT, A NEW MOVEMENT AMONGST MAINSTREAM ECONOMISTS RECENTLY LAUNCHED IN FRANCE BY DRS CAHUC AND ZYLBERBERG."

SPEAKING ON BEHALF OF THE WHO, DR. CAHUC EXPLAINED THAT THE VIRUS WORKS BY TURNING OFF THE ONE GENETIC MARKER THAT DISTINGUISHES THIS SPECIES FROM THE REST OF ITS GENUS, THE HUMAN RACE. THIS IS THE SO–CALLED "*MILTON*" GENE (FRIEDMAN, 1953), WHICH GOES DORMANT IN OTHER HUMANS AS THEY PASS THROUGH PUBERTY. ITS INACTIVITY REDUCES THEIR IMAGINATIVE CAPACITY, MAKING IT IMPOSSIBLE FOR THEM TO CONTINUE BELIEVING IN SUCH ENDEARING INFANTILE FANTASIES AS THE TOOTH FAIRY AND SANTA CLAUS. WHILE REGRETTABLE, THIS DROP IN IMAGINATION IS NECESSARY TO PREPARE HUMANS FOR THE ADULT PHASE OF THEIR EXISTENCE.

"PROFESSOR MILTON FRIEDMAN FOUND A WAY TO RE–ACTIVATE THIS GENE DURING PHD TRAINING, USING HIS *AS IF* GENE SPLICING TECHNIQUE", DR. ZYLBERBERG ELABORATED.

..."THIS ENABLED A WONDERFUL OUTPOURING OF IMAGINATIVE BELIEFS BY MAINSTREAM ECONOMISTS, WHICH GAVE BIRTH TO CONCEPTS LIKE NAIRU, MONEY NEUTRALITY, RATIONAL EXPECTATIONS, AND EVENTUALLY EVEN DSGE MODELS. THIS WEALTH OF IMAGINATION WAS REGARDED BY MAINSTREAM ECONOMISTS AS A MORE THAN SUFFICIENT COMPENSATION FOR RETURNING TO THE CHILD-LIKE PHASE OF THE HUMAN SPECIES."

THE **MILTON GENE** CONFERRED OTHER ADVANTAGES ON MAINSTREAM ECONOMISTS, WHICH HAVE BEEN HIGHLY IMPORTANT TO THEIR SUCCESS IN COMPETITION AGAINST THEIR RIVAL SPECIES, THE HETERODOX ECONOMISTS. "BEING ENDOWED WITH A CHILD-LIKE NATURE, THE ARGUMENTS OF MAINSTREAM ECONOMISTS WERE TREATED WITH THE LOW LEVEL OF CRITICAL EVALUATION THAT ADULT HUMANS NORMALLY RESERVE FOR CONVERSATIONS WITH THEIR INFANT STAGE", SAID DR. CAHUC. "THIS MADE THEIR POLICY RECOMMENDATIONS MUCH MORE LIKELY TO BE ADOPTED, INSTEAD OF THE MORE COMPLICATED PROPOSALS PUT FORWARD BY THEIR NICHE RIVALS", HE SAID.

THE NEW VIRUS, NAMED **REALITY**, DE—ACTIVATES THE MILTON GENE ONCE MORE. "CONSEQUENTLY", DR. CAHUC WARNED, "THE VERY BELIEFS THAT DEFINE THIS UNIQUE SPECIES ARE AT RISK. UNLESS WE ARE VERY CAREFUL, IT MAY BECOME EXTINCT!".

UNFORTUNATELY, THERE IS AS YET NO KNOWN CURE TO THIS VIRUS. "WHO THEREFORE RECOMMENDS COMPLETE AVOIDANCE OF 'REALITY' AS THE ONLY EFFECTIVE STRATEGY FOR THOSE WISHING TO REMAIN AS MAINSTREAM ECONOMISTS", DR. CAHUC CONCLUDED.

HOWEVER, THIS STRATEGY IS MADE EXTREMELY DIFFICULT BY ONE CUNNING CHARACTERISTIC OF THE REALITY VIRUS: AFTER AN INITIAL PHASE OF DISORIENTATION AND DISTRESS, ITS SUFFERERS BEGIN TO EXPERIENCE PLEASURE, AND ACTUALLY WANT TO PASS THE **VIRUS** ON TO OTHERS.

"ITS TRANSMISSION MECHANISM IS A PARTICULARLY INSIDIOUS ASPECT OF THIS DISEASE", DR. CAHUC LAMENTED.

THE FIRST CONFIRMED VICTIM AND CARRIER OF THE REALITY VIRUS WAS THE EX–FEDERAL RESERVE OF MINNEAPOLIS PRESIDENT NARAYANA KOCHERLOKOTA, WHO WROTE A BRIEF NOTE PROMISINGLY ENTITLED "TOY MODELS" IN JULY 2016. IT NOW APPEARS THAT THE VERY TITLE OF THE PAPER WAS A DISGUISED MANIFESTATION OF THE DISEASE, SINCE MAINSTREAM ECONOMISTS ENJOY PLAYING WITH BOTH TOYS AND MODELS.

THIS ENABLED IT TO BOND WITH THE RECIPIENTS' MILTON GENE. HAVING PENETRATED THE GENE'S DEFENCES, THE VIRUS STRUCK!

THE PAPER BEGAN INNOCUOUSLY ENOUGH, BY RESTATING THE CONVENTIONAL MAINSTREAM BELIEF THAT "MACROECONOMIC RESEARCH CAN AND SHOULD BE GROUNDED IN AN ESTABLISHED BODY OF THEORY".

BUT THEN, KOCHERLOKOTA CONTINUED THAT:

"MY OWN VIEW IS THAT, AFTER THE HIGHLY SURPRISING NATURE OF THE DATA FLOW OVER THE PAST TEN YEARS, THIS BASIC PREMISE OF "SERIOUS" MODELLING IS WRONG:

WE SIMPLY DO NOT HAVE A SETTLED SUCCESSFUL THEORY OF THE MACROECONOMY.

THE CHOICES MADE 25–40 YEARS AGO – MADE THEN FOR A NUMBER OF EXCELLENT REASONS – SHOULD NOT BE TREATED AS WRITTEN IN STONE OR EVEN IN PEN.

BY DOING SO, WE ARE CHOKING OFF PATHS FOR UNDERSTANDING THE MACROECONOMY."
(KOCHERLAKOTA, "TOY MODELS", JULY 14 2016)

OUTBREAK

THE WHO'S HOPES THAT THIS OUTBREAK WAS CONFINED TO THE USA'S FRESHWATER SYSTEM WERE DASHED JUST A MONTH LATER, WHEN THE PREVIOUSLY HIGHLY RESISTANT SALTWATER ECONOMIST **OLIVIER BLANCHARD** SHOWED SIGNS OF INFECTION.

UNDER THE COVER OF A RESPECTED MAINSTREAM OUTLET, BLANCHARD RELEASED A PAPER WITH THE WORRYING TITLE OF **"DO DSGE MODELS HAVE A FUTURE?"**.

THOUGH THE PAPER THANKFULLY CONCLUDED THAT THEY DO, IT MADE A NUMBER OF POTENTIALLY VIRALLY—INFLUENCED STATEMENTS, SUCH AS...

"THERE ARE MANY REASONS TO DISLIKE CURRENT DSGE MODELS."

"FIRST: THEY ARE BASED ON UNAPPEALING ASSUMPTIONS. NOT JUST SIMPLIFYING ASSUMPTIONS, AS ANY MODEL MUST, BUT ASSUMPTIONS PROFOUNDLY AT ODDS WITH WHAT WE KNOW ABOUT CONSUMERS AND FIRMS." (BLANCHARD, 2016, P. 1)

"THIS IS A VERY TROUBLING ASSERTION", DR. ZYLBERBERG STATED, "SINCE IN THE PAST BLANCHARD HAD NO DIFFICULTY IN MAKING **AS IF** ASSUMPTIONS ABOUT THINGS THAT WERE REALLY **AS ISN'T**."

INITIALLY THE WHO THOUGHT THAT BLANCHARD MAY HAVE ACQUIRED THE VIRUS FROM KOCHERLOKOTA, BUT FURTHER RESEARCH IMPLIES THAT BLANCHARD COULD HIMSELF HAVE BEEN THE ORIGINAL SOURCE OF THE VIRUS.

DR. ZYLBERBERG NOTED THAT BLANCHARD CLEARLY HAD A STRONG IMMUNE SYSTEM, GIVEN SUCH SUPERBLY IMAGINATIVE PAPERS AS "THE STATE OF MACRO" (BLANCHARD, AUGUST 2008), IN WHICH HE REMARKED, ONE YEAR AFTER THE START OF THE GLOBAL FINANCIAL CRISIS, THAT "THE STATE OF MACRO IS GOOD" (BLANCHARD, 2009, P. 210).

HOWEVER, EPIDEMIOLOGICAL RESEARCH BY DR. CAHUC REVEALED THAT THERE WERE SIGNS OF INFECTION AS LONG AGO AS 2010, WHEN BLANCHARD WROTE THAT:

"IT WAS TEMPTING FOR MACROECONOMISTS AND POLICYMAKERS ALIKE TO TAKE MUCH OF THE CREDIT FOR THE STEADY DECREASE IN CYCLICAL FLUCTUATIONS FROM THE EARLY 1980S ON AND TO CONCLUDE THAT WE KNEW HOW TO CON—DUCT MACROECONOMIC POLICY.

WE DID NOT RESIST TEMPTATION. THE CRISIS CLEARLY FORCES US TO QUESTION OUR EARLIER ASSESSMENT." (BLANCHARD ET AL., 2010, P. 199)

THIS WAS FOLLOWED UP BY A 2014 PAPER IN WHICH THE DISORIENTATION STAGE OF THE VIRUS WAS EVIDENT. ENTITLED *"WHERE DANGER LURKS"* (BLANCHARD, 2014), THIS PAPER ASSERTED THAT:

UNTIL THE 2008 GLOBAL FINANCIAL CRISIS, MAINSTREAM U.S. MACRO-ECONOMICS HAD TAKEN AN INCREASINGLY BENIGN VIEW OF ECONOMIC FLUCTUATIONS IN OUTPUT AND EMPLOYMENT.

THE CRISIS HAS MADE IT CLEAR THAT THIS VIEW WAS WRONG AND THAT THERE IS A NEED FOR A DEEP REASSESSMENT. (BLANCHARD, 2014, P. 28)

THE WHO WOULD HAVE RAISED AN ALARM ABOUT BLANCHARD CASE EARLIER, WERE IT NOT FOR THE SOOTHING CONCLUSION TO THIS PAPER, WHICH WAS THAT:

THE CRISIS HAS BEEN IMMENSELY PAINFUL. BUT ONE OF ITS SILVER LININGS HAS BEEN TO JOLT MACROECONOMICS AND MACROECONOMIC POLICY. THE MAIN POLICY LESSON IS A SIMPLE ONE...

STAY AWAY FROM DARK CORNERS. (BLANCHARD, 2014, P. 31)

IT WAS CLEAR FROM THIS THAT BLANCHARD'S MILTON GENE WAS STILL ACTIVE, DR. CAHUC NOTED, SINCE MAINSTREAM ECONOMICS ACTUALLY PROVIDES NO WAY TO IDENTIFY WHERE THE DARK CORNERS ARE.

THE WHO NOW DEEPLY REGRETS ITS EARLY COMPLACENCY, SINCE ALMOST IMMEDIATELY AFTER BLANCHARD'S 2016 OUTBREAK, AN EVEN MORE VIRULENT STRAIN OF THE VIRUS APPEARED: THE *"RR"* OR *"ROMER REALITY"* VARIANT. THIS AGGRESSIVE VIRUS BROKE INTO THE WILD ON SEPTEMBER 14, 2016, WHEN A PAPER WAS ACCIDENTALLY RELEASED FROM THE ISOLATION WARD AT YALE UNIVERSITY. THIS STRAIN OF THE VIRUS APPARENTLY HAS NO NEED TO CONCEAL ITS PURPOSE, SINCE THE PAPER WAS ENTITLED, *"THE TROUBLE WITH MACROECONOMICS"* AND IT MADE MANY ASSERTIONS THAT INDICATE THAT THE SUFFERER'S MILTON GENE HAS BEEN COMPLETELY SILENCED.

"NOT ONLY DOES IT BLUNTLY ASSERT IN ITS ABSTRACT THAT 'FOR MORE THAN THREE DECADES, MACROECONOMICS HAS GONE BACKWARDS'", DR. ZYLBERBERG NOTED, "IT EVEN PARODIES MAINSTREAM ECONOMICS IN A WAY THAT WE THOUGHT WAS PREVIOUSLY CONFINED TO THE '*KK*' (KEEN AT KINGSTON; KEEN, 2011) VIRUS, TO WHICH MAINSTREAM ECONOMISTS HAD PREVIOUSLY BEEN COMPLETELY RESISTANT".

MAINSTREAM ECONOMISTS ARE ADVISED TO COMPLETELY AVOID CONTACT WITH CARRIERS OF THE **RR** STRAIN, SINCE IT MAKES A FRONTAL ASSAULT ON THE MILTON GENE ITSELF — SEEKING NOT MERELY TO DE-ACTIVATE IT, BUT TO REMOVE IT ENTIRELY FROM THE GENOME WITH OUTRAGEOUS STATEMENTS LIKE THE FOLLOWING:

IN RESPONSE TO THE OBSERVATION THAT THE SHOCKS ARE IMAGINARY, A STANDARD DEFENSE INVOKES MILTON FRIEDMAN'S (1953) METHODOLOGICAL ASSERTION FROM UNNAMED AUTHORITY THAT "THE MORE SIGNIFICANT THE THEORY, THE MORE UNREALISTIC THE ASSUMPTIONS (P.14)." MORE RECENTLY, "ALL MODELS ARE FALSE" SEEMS TO HAVE BECOME THE UNIVERSAL HAND-WAVE FOR DISMISSING ANY FACT THAT DOES NOT CONFORM TO THE MODEL THAT IS THE CURRENT FAVOURITE. THE NONCOMMITTAL RELATIONSHIP WITH THE TRUTH REVEALED BY THESE METHODOLOGICAL EVASIONS AND THE "LESS THAN TOTALLY CONVINCED ..." DISMISSAL OF FACT GOES SO FAR BEYOND POST-MODERN IRONY THAT IT DESERVES ITS OWN LABEL. I SUGGEST "POST-REAL." (ROMER, 2016, P. 5)

"WORSE STILL", NOTED DR. CAHUC, "IT IDENTIFIES MAINSTREAM ECONOMIC BELIEFS — WHICH ADULT HUMANS BELIEVE ARE SCIENTIFIC CONCEPTS, AND THEREFORE TO BE TAKEN SERIOUSLY — WITH OTHER BELIEFS THAT ADULTS THEMSELVES ONCE HAD IN THEIR YOUTH, AND WHICH THEY THEREFORE KNOW ARE FANTASIES."

"THIS COULD MEAN THAT ADULT HUMANS — AND IN PARTICULAR, POLITICIANS — MIGHT START TO REJECT MAINSTREAM ECONOMIC ADVICE," DR ZYLBERBERG INTERJECTED.

"THIS COULD BE FATAL TO THE CONTINUED EXISTENCE OF MAIN-STREAM ECONOMISTS. THE THREAT IS THAT SERIOUS."

IT ALSO PARODIES GREAT MAINSTREAM ECONOMICS WORKS OF IMAGINATION LIKE "SHOCKS AND FRICTIONS IN U.S. BUSINESS CYCLES: A BAYESIAN DSGE APPROACH" BY THE RENOWNED **SMETS** AND **WOUTERS** (SMETS AND WOUTERS, 2007):

WHAT MATTERS IN THE MODEL IS NOT MONEY BUT THE IMAGINARY FORCES. HERE IS WHAT THE AUTHORS SAY ABOUT THEM, MODIFIED ONLY WITH INSERTIONS IN BOLD AND THE ABBREVIATION "AKA" AS A STAND IN FOR "ALSO KNOWN AS."

WHILE "DEMAND" SHOCKS SUCH AS THE **AETHER** AKA RISK PREMIUM, EXOGENOUS SPENDING, AND INVESTMENT-SPECIFIC **PHLOGISTON** AKA TECHNOLOGY SHOCKS EXPLAIN A SIGNIFICANT FRACTION OF THE SHORT-RUN FORECAST VARIANCE IN OUTPUT, BOTH THE **TROLL'S WAGE** MARK-UP (OR CALORIC AKA LABOR SUPPLY) AND, TO A LESSER EXTENT, OUTPUT-SPECIFIC **PHLOGISTON** AKA TECHNOLOGY SHOCKS EXPLAIN MOST OF ITS VARIATION IN THE MEDIUM TO LONG RUN....THIRD, INFLATION DEVELOPMENTS ARE MOSTLY DRIVEN BY THE GREMLIN'S PRICE MARK-UP SHOCKS IN THE SHORT RUN AND THE TROLL'S WAGE MARK-UP SHOCKS IN THE LONG RUN.

A COMMENT IN A SUBSEQUENT PAPER (LINDE, SMETS, WOUTERS 2016, FOOTNOTE 16) UNDERLINES THE FLEXIBILITY THAT IMAGINARY DRIVING FORCES BRING TO POST-REAL MACROECONOMICS (ONCE AGAIN WITH MY ADDITIONS IN BOLD):

THE PROMINENT ROLE OF THE **GREMLIN'S** PRICE AND THE **TROLL'S** WAGE MARKUP FOR EXPLAINING INFLATION AND BEHAVIOUR OF REAL WAGES IN THE SW-MODEL HAVE BEEN CRITICIZED BY CHARI, KEHOE AND MCGRATTAN (2009) AS IMPLAUSIBLY LARGE. GALÍ, SMETS AND WOUTERS (2011), HOWEVER, SHOWS THAT THE SIZE OF THE MARKUP SHOCKS CAN BE REDUCED SUBSTANTIALLY BY ALLOWING FOR **CALORIC** AKA PREFERENCE SHOCKS TO HOUSEHOLD PREFERENCES. (ROMER, 2016, P. 7-8)

THE DANGERS TO MAINSTREAM ECONOMISTS ARE THEREFORE CLEAR: AVOID 'REALITY' AT ALL COSTS, IF YOU WANT TO REMAIN MAINSTREAM ECONOMISTS.

THOUGH VERY CONCERNED, DRS. CAHUC AND ZYLBERBERG DO TAKE SOLACE THAT THE **RR** STRAIN OF THE VIRUS HAS RECENTLY BEEN MOVED FROM YALE UNIVERSITY,...

...WHERE IT COULD EASILY COME IN CONTACT WITH MANY ACADEMIC MAINSTREAM ECONOMISTS, TO THE WORLD BANK. "THANKFULLY, THIS WILL ISOLATE THE **ROMER REALITY** STRAND FROM ACADEMIC ECONOMICS DEPARTMENTS, WHERE MAINSTREAM ECONOMISTS BREED. THERE IS THEREFORE STILL HOPE FOR THE SURVIVAL OF THIS SPECIES," DR. CAHUC CONCLUDED.

Catalog of Viral Symptoms

BLANCHARD, O. 2009. THE STATE OF MACRO. ANNUAL REVIEW OF ECONOMICS, 1, 209–228.

BLANCHARD, O. 2014. WHERE DANGER LURKS. FINANCE & DEVELOPMENT, 51.

BLANCHARD, O. 2016. DO DSGE MODELS HAVE A FUTURE? [ONLINE]. PETERSON INSTITUTE FOR INTERNATIONAL ECONOMICS. AVAILABLE: HTTPS://PIIE.COM/SYSTEM/FILES/DOCUMENTS/PB16–11.PDF.

BLANCHARD, O., DELL'ARICCIA, G. & MAURO, P. 2010. RETHINKING MACROECONOMIC POLICY. JOURNAL OF MONEY, CREDIT, AND BANKING, 42, 199–215.

KEEN, S. 2011. DEBUNKING ECONOMICS: THE NAKED EMPEROR DETHRONED?, LONDON, ZED BOOKS.

KOCHERLAKOTA, N. 2016. TOY MODELS [ONLINE]. AVAILABLE: HTTPS://DOCS.GOOGLE.COM/VIEWER?A=V&PID=SITES&SRCID=ZGVMYXVS-DGRVBWFPBNXRB2NOZXJSYWTVDGEWMDL8 Z3G6MTAYZMIZODCXNGZIOGY4YG.

ROMER, P. 2016. THE TROUBLE WITH MACROECONOMICS.

BIBLIOGRAPHY

CAHUC, P. & ZYLBERBERG, A. 2016. LE NÉGATIONNISME ÉCONOMIQUE ET COMMENT S'EN DÉBARRASSER, PARIS, FLAMMARION.

FRIEDMAN, M. 1953. THE METHODOLOGY OF POSITIVE ECONOMICS. ESSAYS IN POSITIVE ECONOMICS. CHICAGO: UNIVERSITY OF CHICAGO PRESS.

SMETS, F. & WOUTERS, R. 2007. SHOCKS AND FRICTIONS IN US BUSINESS CYCLES: A BAYESIAN DSGE APPROACH. AMERICAN ECONOMIC REVIEW, 97, 586–606.

ECONOMICS SHOULD NOT BE A LAUGHING MATTER. I HOPE YOU GET SOME LAUGHS OUT OF THE THREE SATIRES IN THIS BOOK. BUT ECONOMICS SHOULD NOT REALLY BE A LAUGHING MATTER. IT SHOULD INSTEAD BE A WAY TO UNDERSTAND, AND MANAGE, THE COMPLEX ECONOMY IN WHICH WE LIVE.

THE FACT THAT IT ISN'T WHAT IT SHOULD BE IS OBVIOUS AFTER THE FINANCIAL CRISIS OF 2008, WHICH TOOK MAINSTREAM ECONOMISTS ENTIRELY BY SURPRISE. IN ITS AFTERMATH, INEQUALITY HAS BEEN MADE EVEN WORSE BY GOVERNMENT AND CENTRAL BANK POLICIES THAT DID MORE TO RESCUE WALL STREET THAN MAIN STREET.

A REALISTIC ECONOMICS WOULD NOT MERELY HAVE SEEN THE CRISIS COMING, IT WOULD HAVE HELPED US PREVENT IT. A REALISTIC ECONOMICS WOULD NOT HAVE MADE EXTREME INEQUALITY, ONE OF THE FUNDAMENTAL PROBLEMS OF OUR TIME, EVEN WORSE.

SO I HOPE YOU'LL BE MAD AS WELL AS AMUSED BY THE TIME YOU FINISH READING THESE SATIRES, AND THAT YOU'LL WANT TO KNOW "WHAT CAN I DO TO HELP?"

AS I NOTE ON THE BACK PAGE, YOU CAN HELP BY SUPPORTING MY CAMPAIGN TO REBUILD ECONOMICS VIA PATREON (SEE HTTPS://WWW.PATREON.COM/PROFSTEVE-KEEN).

BUT THERE ARE OTHER WAYS TO GET INVOLVED AS WELL. TWO OF THE KEY GROUPS THAT ARE TRYING TO DR AG ECONOMICS OUT OF ITS MYTHS AND INTO THE REAL WORLD ARE THE STUDENT GROUP RETHINKING ECONOMICS: HTTP://WWW.RETHINKECONOMICS.ORG/, AND THE PROMOTING ECONOMIC PLURALISM MOVEMENT: HTTPS://WWW.ECONOMICPLURALISM.ORG/.

GET IN TOUCH AND HELP THEM MAKE ECONOMICS FIT FOR PURPOSE.

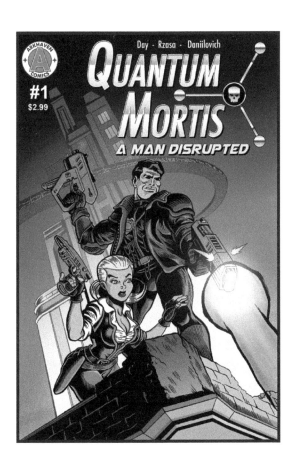

Lightning Source UK Ltd.
Milton Keynes UK
UKHW05f1734140318
319428UK00003B/39/P